# COOKING WITH HERBS AND SPICES

**Sian Llewellyn**

DOMINO BOOKS LTD

## METRIC/IMPERIAL/AMERICAN UNITS

We are all used to doubling or halving a recipe. Thus, a Victoria sandwich may be made using 4 oz each of flour, sugar and butter with 2 eggs or 6 oz each of flour, sugar and butter with 3 eggs. The proportions of the ingredients are unchanged. This must be so for all units. Use either the metric units or the imperial units given in the recipes, do not mix the two.

It is not practical to give the exact equivalents of metric and imperial units because 1 oz equals 28.35 gm and 1 pint equals 568 ml. The tables on page 47 indicate suitable quantities but liquids should be carefully added to obtain the correct consistency. See also the charts on page iv.

## PINTS TO MILLILITRES AND LITRES

**The following are approximations only**

¼ pint = 150 ml
½ pint = 275 ml
¾ pint = 425 ml

1 pint = 575 ml
1¾ pints = 1000 ml (1 litre)
3 pints = 1½ litres

# CONTENTS




Cover photograph by Michael Corrin

ISBN 1 85122 085 2

The following charts give the approximate equivalents for metric and imperial weights, and oven temperatures.

| Ounces | Approx gm to nearest whole number | Approx gm to nearest whole 25 gm |
|---|---|---|
| 1 | 28 | 25 |
| 2 | 57 | 50 |
| 3 | 85 | 75 |
| 4 | 113 | 125 |
| 5 | 142 | 150 |
| 6 | 170 | 175 |
| 7 | 198 | 200 |
| 8 | 226 | 225 |
| 9 | 255 | 250 |
| 10 | 283 | 275 |
| 11 | 311 | 300 |
| 12 | 340 | 350 |
| 13 | 368 | 375 |
| 14 | 396 | 400 |
| 15 | 428 | 425 |
| 16 | 456 | 450 |

**OVEN TEMPERATURE GUIDE**

| | Electricity °C | Electricity °F | Gas Mark |
|---|---|---|---|
| Very cool | 110 | 225 | ¼ |
| | 130 | 250 | ½ |
| Cool | 140 | 275 | 1 |
| | 150 | 300 | 2 |
| Moderate | 170 | 325 | 3 |
| | 180 | 350 | 4 |
| Moderately hot | 190 | 375 | 5 |
| | 200 | 400 | 6 |
| Hot | 220 | 425 | 7 |
| | 230 | 450 | 8 |
| Very hot | 240 | 475 | 9 |

When using this chart for weights over 16 ounces, add the appropriate figures in the column giving the nearest whole number of grammes and then adjust to the nearest unit of 25. For example, 18 oz (16 oz + 2 oz) becomes 456 + 57 = 513 to the nearest whole number and 500 gm to the nearest unit of 25.
Throughout the book, 1 teaspoon = 5 ml and 1 tablespoon = 15 ml.

# TO USE HERBS AND SPICES

Herbs and spices should be used sparingly, to complement and to bring out the natural flavour of foods. At first do not use more than a quarter teaspoonful of any one dried herb or spice or a half teaspoonful of dried mixed herbs in a dish to serve four. Dried herbs tend to be three or four times as strong as the fresh kind. If possible use herbs and spices for only one dish at a meal. The more the herbs are crushed or broken up, the better their fragrance is released. Sometimes herbs may be blended with butter before being added to the dish. Herbs should be added to soups just before cooking is complete - as a bunch tied together, a *bouquet garni,* or in a little muslin bag with a few peppercorns. The *bouquet* is removed before serving.

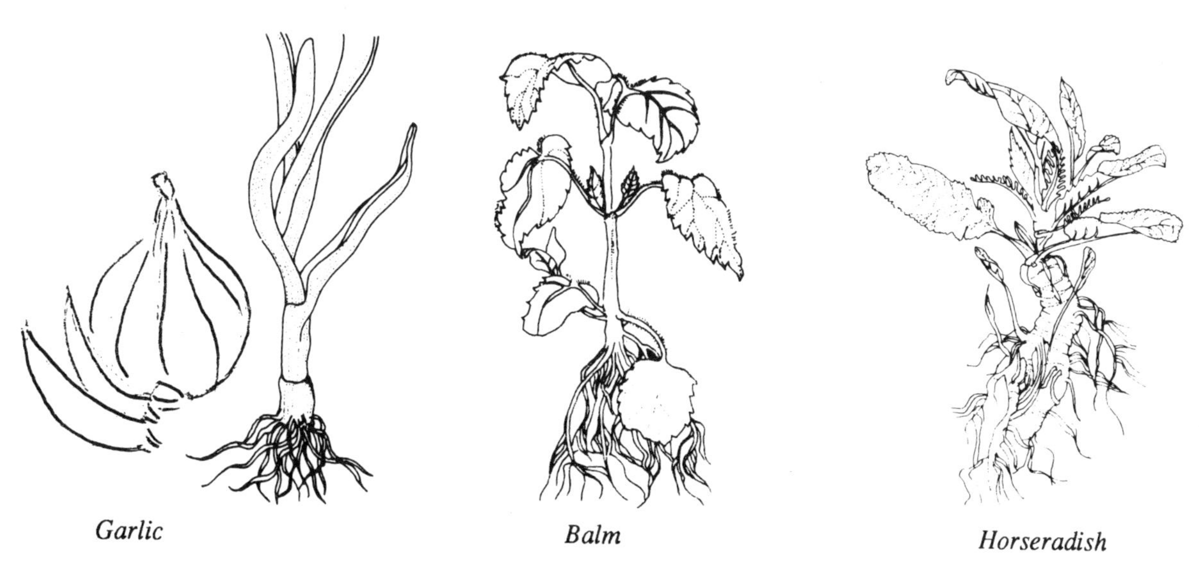

*Garlic* *Balm* *Horseradish*

# TO PRESERVE AND STORE HERBS AND SPICES

Only pick as much of a herb that can be used at one time. If the leaves are needed, if possible, pick them before the flowers form to obtain the best flavour. Large leaves may be cut individually but for small leaves, it is necessary to cut the stems. Herbs are best picked on a dry day in mid morning, after the dew has dried but the sun is not too hot.

**To Dry** If necessary, wash the herbs in cold running water, shake and pat dry. Tie two or three sprigs together and hang in a warm, dry place such as an airing cupboard. If the bunches are laid on shelves, turn the herbs regularly. Allow two to three weeks for drying in this way. The herbs can be dried quickly by placing in front of a cool oven but they should be cooled before storing.

**Seeds** should be collected when the heads of the plant have turned brown but before they scatter - as for caraway, coriander, dill, fennel and lovage.

**Chamomile flowers** used for making tea and pot-pourri should be picked before they are fully open. Hang in bunches until dry and then strip off the flowers to store in airtight jars.

**Parsley** should be plunged into boiling water to which a pinch of bicarbonate of soda has been added. The herb is then patted dry and placed on trays outside the oven which is set at 121°C - 129°C (250°F - 2750°F, gas mark ½ - 1) until it is crisp.

**Garlic** should be picked in the autumn and stored in a cool, airy place and treated in the same way as onions.

**To Store** Leaves that are brittle when dry can be rubbed off easily, powdered with a rolling pin, and rubbed through a fine hair sieve. Dried herbs should be kept in airtight jars in a dark cool place. Dried herbs and seeds may be used for a year and some retain their fragrance for even longer. Spices should be stored in dry, airtight containers and should be bought in small quantities.

**To Freeze** Some herbs, such as chives, mint or borage, or parsley can be stored in the freezer. Snip the chives, chop the mint or borage or parsley, place in ice cube trays, fill with cold water and freeze. This is a convenient form of storage for use in drinks, soups or casseroles. Sprigs or leaves may be wrapped in foil, making sure that all air has been expelled, and then frozen. Herbs in the freezer will usually keep for six months or more.

# COOKING WITH HERBS AND SPICES

Certain herbs have become traditionally associated with particular foods. A *bouquet garni* for soups, *auxfine herbes* for egg dishes and a handful of herbs for salads make all the difference. NB only one, two or at the most three herbs should be used at the same time.

**Bouquet Garni** Small bunch of herbs, usually a mixture of parsley stems, thyme and a bay leaf, tied in a muslin bag. This is left in the dish during cooking and removed before the dish is served.

**SOUPS** Fresh herbs are very good garnishes. Finely chopped parsley or chervil can be used with most soups, chopped chives or celery leaves with meat soups; chopped dill or fennel with fish soups. Pepper, mustard and cinnamon also add distinctive flavours.

| | |
|---|---|
| Beef | Basil or marjoram may be included in the *bouquet garni.* |
| Chicken | Add tarragon, marjoram, sage and rosemary to the soup or add sage to the *bouquet garni.* |
| Lamb | Include mint, rosemary or dill in the *bouquet garni..* |
| Mixed Vegetable | Any two of the following may be included in the *bouquet garni* - basil, celery, dill, marjoram, parsley, rosemary, sage, tarragon, thyme. |
| Consommé | Include a sprig of tarragon in the *bouquet garni.* |
| Pea | Include mint or savory in the *bouquet garni.* |
| Tomato | Include a sprig of basil, mint or marjoram in the *bouquet garni.* |

**FISH** Celery, chervil and parsley are good with delicately flavoured fish and shellfish: basil, bay, dill, fennel, marjoram, rosemary, sage, tarragon and thyme are good with stronger flavoured fish.

| | |
|---|---|
| Cod | Garlic, oregano, parsley. |

| | |
|---|---|
| Haddock | Bay, celery, garlic, parsley, thyme. |
| Hake | Celery, chervil, parsley. |
| Halibut | Basil, bay, dill. |
| Lemon Sole | Celery, parsley, savory. |
| Plaice | Savory, celery. |
| Shellfish | Bay, garlic, oregano. |

**MEAT** Herbs may be used to enhance the flavour of meat by sprinkling them over the meat or using them in stuffings or accompanying sauces or in herb butters. Spices, especially mustard and peppers, add to the flavour of meat dishes.

| | |
|---|---|
| Beef | Curry powder, basil, horseradish, marjoram, mustard, rosemary, thyme.<br>Casseroles and stews - *bouquet garni.*<br>Goulash - caraway seeds.<br>Steak - tarragon, parsley.<br>Steak and kidney pudding - ground coriander. |
| Kidneys | Parsley. |
| Lamb | Bay, dill, garlic, mint (as mint sauce), rosemary. |
| Liver | Bay, celery leaves, garlic, parsley, rosemary, sage. |
| Pork | Basil, bay, chives, rosemary, sage, thyme, parsley. |
| Veal | Parsley, rosemary, sage, thyme. |
| Stews | Bay, chives, dill, garlic, horseradish, marjoram, parsley, rosemary, tarragon, thyme. |

**POULTRY and GAME** Herbs and spices may be introduced by sprinkling them over the meat or in stuffings and accompanying sauces.

| | |
|---|---|
| Chicken | Basil, celery, celery leaves, dill, fennel, garlic. |
| Duck | Basil, celery leaves, marjoram, parsley, rosemary, sage, thyme. |

| | |
|---|---|
| Goose | Basil, bay, garlic, rosemary, sage, tarragon. |
| Partridge | *Bouquet garni,* chervil, chives, marjoram, rosemary, thyme. |
| Pheasant | *Bouquet garni,* celery. |
| Venison | Usually marinated and marinade may be seasoned with a *bouquet garni*, celery leaves, juniper berries, rosemary, sage. |
| **VEGETABLES and SALADS** | Herbs should be used lightly for cooking vegetables or sprinkling over salads. |
| Beans | Sage, summer savory, parsley. |
| Beetroot | Chives, tarragon or parsley with beetroot salad. |
| Cabbage | Parsley, caraway. |
| Carrots | Basil, mint, parsley, summer savory. |
| Peas | Mint, parsley, summer savory. |
| Potatoes | Chives, garlic, mint, parsley. |
| Spinach | Mint. |
| Tomatoes | Balm, basil, chives, marjoram, mint, parsley. |
| Green Salads | Angelica leaves, balm, borage, chervil, chives, dill foliage, fennel, garlic, sage, salad burnet, tarragon, thyme. |
| **EGGS** | Basil, chervil, chives, curry powder, lovage, mace, marjoram, nutmeg, parsley, salad burnet, tarragon. |
| **HARD CHEESES** | Basil, chervil, sage, thyme. |
| **SOFT CHEESES** | Basil, caraway, chives, curry powder, dill, garlic, mint, parsley, sage. |

| | |
|---|---|
| **SAUCES** | Angelica leaves, bay, chervil, dill, fennel, garlic, horseradish, mint, mustard, parsley. |
| **HERB BUTTERS** | Chervil, parsley, shallots, tarragon. |
| **STUFFINGS** | The herbs used depend on the meat. |
| **BISCUITS and CAKES** | Allspice, bay, basil, caraway, cinnamon, cloves, coriander, ginger, rosemary, sesame, vanilla. |
| **DESSERTS** | Angelica, bay, caraway, cinnamon, cloves, dill, ginger, mace, mint, nutmeg, sesame, tansy, vanilla. |
| **JAMS and JELLIES** | Mint, parsley. |
| **DRINKS** | Balm, bergamot and flowers, borage and flowers, cinnamon, lovage, mint, rosemary, salad burnet. |
| **VINEGAR** | Allspice, basil, chervil, dill, marjoram, tarragon, thyme. |
| **TEAS** | Chamomile, dill, mint, parsley. |
| **GARNISHES** | Angelica, balm, basil, bergamot flowers, borage flowers, chervil, chives, mint, parsley, rosemary, savory, thyme. |

# SOLE IN WHITE WINE

| METRIC | IMPERIAL |
|---|---|
| *2 soles* | *2 soles* |
| *50 gm butter* | *2 oz butter* |
| *12 gm flour* | *½ oz flour* |
| *2 egg yolks* | *2 egg yolks* |
| *50 gm shrimps* | *2 oz shrimps* |
| *250 ml white wine* | *½ pint white wine* |
| *parsley* | *parsley* |
| *salt and pepper* | *salt and pepper* |

Clean, skin and fillet the fish. Pat dry and season. Roll up the fillets and place in an ovenproof dish. Dot with half the butter and pour half the wine over the fish. Cover and bake in the centre of a moderate oven (180°C, 350°F, gas mark 4) for 20 minutes. Remove the fish on to a dish and keep warm. Decant the wine liquor and make up to 250 ml (½ pint) with more wine. Melt half the remaining butter in a saucepan and stir in the flour using a wooden spoon. Work in the wine. Cook gently for 2 - 3 minutes. Remove from the heat and beat in the egg yolks and the remaining butter. Season, re-heat, but do not boil. Pour over the fish. Garnish with shrimps and parsley.

# BAKED STUFFED FISH

METRIC
*4 fillets of sole - skinned*
*or 4 cod steaks*
*50 gm butter*
*4 rashers bacon*
*salt and pepper*
*celery stuffing*

IMPERIAL
*4 fillets of sole - skinned*
*or 4 cod steaks*
*2 oz butter*
*4 rashers bacon*
*salt and pepper*
*celery stuffing*

Wash and dry the fish. Place a portion of the celery stuffing on each fillet of sole, roll up and secure with a cocktail stick or cut each cod steak, insert the stuffing and secure. Melt the butter and coat the fish. Lay the fish in a roasting pan, season and cover each with a rasher of bacon. Bake in a moderate oven (180°C, 350°F, gas mark 4) for 40 - 60 minutes until the flesh flakes away. If the fish becomes too dry, baste with the juices in the pan or a little more melted butter. Serve with green salad.
**Celery stuffing:** See page 21.

# CREAM OF TOMATO SOUP

METRIC
*1 kg tomatoes*
*1 small onion*
*1 bay leaf*
*pinch pepper, cinnamon, cloves, salt*
*25 gm butter*
*2 tablespoons flour*
*500 ml milk*

IMPERIAL
*2 lb tomatoes*
*1 small onion*
*1 bay leaf*
*pinch pepper, cinnamon, cloves, salt*
*1 oz butter*
*2 tablespoons flour*
*1 pint milk*

Wash and halve the tomatoes. Remove the pulp and press through a sieve to remove the seeds. Purée the pulp. Skin and slice the onion and fry in the butter until softened. Allow the pan to cool slightly and add the milk, stirring to avoid the formation of lumps. Return to the heat and bring to the boil. Add the tomato purée and seasonings. Cover the pan and simmer gently for 30 minutes. Serve with cream.

# CARAWAY SOUP

METRIC
*1 litre chicken stock*
*25 gm butter*
*25 gm flour*
*50 gm finely chopped caraway leaves*
*50 gm coarsely chopped caraway leaves*
*1 egg yolk*
*2 tablespoons cream*
*salt and pepper*
*poached eggs (optional)*

IMPERIAL
*2 pints chicken stock*
*1 oz butter*
*1 oz flour*
*2 oz finely chopped caraway leaves*
*2 oz coarsely chopped caraway leaves*
*1 egg yolk*
*2 tablespoons cream*
*salt and pepper*
*poached eggs (optional)*

Melt the butter and stir in the flour using a wooden spoon. Warm gently for 1 minute and then add the finely chopped caraway leaves. Slowly add the stock, stirring continuously to prevent the formation of lumps. Simmer gently for 5 minutes. Remove from the heat. Beat the cream and egg yolk. Pour a little of the soup into the cream mixture. Blend well and return to the soup in the saucepan. Add the rest of the caraway leaves and salt and pepper to taste. Reheat but do not allow to boil. Serve with poached eggs if liked and buttered toast.

# SPICED BAKED HAM

METRIC
*2 kilos ham joint*
*2 tablespoons honey*
*1 teaspoon dry mustard*
*4 tablespoons brown sugar*
*cloves*

IMPERIAL
*4 lb ham joint*
*2 tablespoons honey*
*1 teaspoon dry mustard*
*4 tablespoons brown sugar*
*cloves*

Soak the ham joint in cold water overnight. Place in a large saucepan and cover with fresh, cold water. Bring to the boil and skim any fat from surface. Simmer, allowing 10 minutes per 500 gm (10 minutes per lb). Remove the ham to a roasting tin. Cut off the rind and score the fat diagonally into a diamond pattern. Mix the honey, sugar and mustard together and brush the ham with the mixture. Stud the diamond fat shapes with cloves. Cook uncovered in the centre of a fairly hot oven (200°C, 400°F, gas mark 6) for 1 hour, basting every 15 minutes. Serve with Cumberland sauce.

# CUMBERLAND SAUCE

METRIC
*4 tablespoons redcurrant jelly*
*4 tablespoons port*
*1 orange*
*1 lemon*
*1 teaspoon each mustard powder, ground ginger*

IMPERIAL
*4 tablespoons redcurrant jelly*
*4 tablespoons port*
*1 orange*
*1 lemon*
*1 teaspoon each mustard powder, ground ginger*

Thinly pare the rinds of the lemon and orange. Cut into small strips and boil in water for 5 minutes. Drain. Place the redcurrant jelly and port in a saucepan and heat to melt the jelly. Mix the mustard and ginger with the juice from half the lemon. Add the juice from the orange, the port and redcurrant jelly and strips of orange and lemon rind. Mix well. Serve cold.

# BRANDY STEAK

METRIC
*250 gm sirloin steak*
*50 gm butter*
*1 tablespoon brandy*
*2 tablespoons sherry*
*1 tablespoon butter creamed with*
*1 teaspoon chopped chives*
*1 tablespoon cream (optional)*

IMPERIAL
*8 oz sirloin steak*
*2 oz butter*
*1 tablespoon brandy*
*2 tablespoons sherry*
*1 tablespoon butter creamed with*
*1 teaspoon chopped chives*
*1 tablespoon cream (optional)*

Melt the butter in a frying pan and cook the steak. Add the brandy and flame. Add the sherry and butter with chives. Serve with creamed or jacket potatoes and green vegetables, pouring the liquor from the pan over the meat. If used, stir the cream into the liquor from the pan when the meat has been removed. Warm but do not boil.

# STEAK AU POIVRE

Crush 2 tablespoons black or green peppercorns using a pestle and mortar or in a polythene bag on a board using a rolling pin. Press the steak on the pepper so that the surfaces become covered with pepper. Cook as in the recipe for brandy steak above but omit the butter creamed with chopped chives.

# HERB BARBECUED CHICKEN

METRIC
*The chicken - jointed*
***The sauce***
*6 tablespoons salad oil*
*3 tablespoons olive oil*
*3 tablespoons lemon juice*
*½ teaspoon salt*
*Pinch each marjoram,*
*thyme, aromat, black pepper*
*pinch oregano*

IMPERIAL
*The chicken - jointed*
***The sauce***
*6 tablespoons salad oil*
*3 tablespoons olive oil*
*3 tablespoons lemon juice*
*½ teaspoon salt*
*Pinch each marjoram,*
*thyme, aromat, black pepper*
*pinch oregano*

Thoroughly mix all the ingredients for the sauce and leave to stand in a cool place for several hours. Coat the chicken joints with the sauce to barbecue or grill.

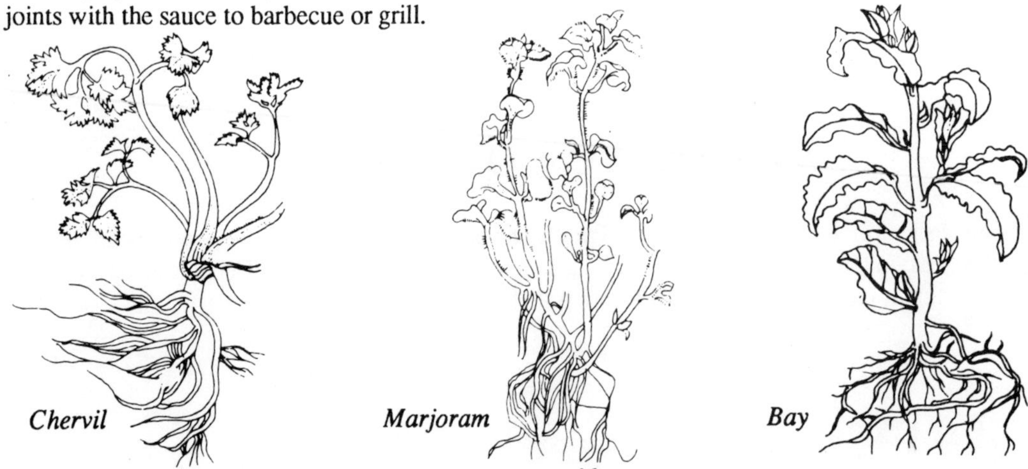

# COQ AU VIN

METRIC
*One 1200 gm chicken*
*100 gm streaky bacon*
*75 gm butter*
*25 gm flour*
*4 medium sized onions*
*100 gm mushrooms*
*1 bayleaf*
*1 sprig parsley*
*1 sprig thyme*
*250 ml Burgundy or other red wine*
*salt and pepper*

IMPERIAL
*One 3 lb chicken*
*4 oz streaky bacon*
*3 oz butter*
*1 oz flour*
*4 medium sized onions*
*4 oz mushrooms*
*1 bayleaf*
*1 sprig parsley*
*1 sprig thyme*
*½ pint Burgundy or other red wine*
*salt and pepper*

Wash, clean and joint the chicken. Remove the rind from the bacon and cut up the bacon. Skin and slice the onions. Melt 50 gm (2 oz) of the butter and fry the bacon and onions until the onions are soft. Place in an ovenproof dish. Fry the chicken joints until brown. Prepare the mushrooms. Tie the herbs in a muslin bag. Place the chicken, mushrooms and herbs in the dish. Season with salt and pepper. Cook in a moderate oven (180°C, 350°F, gas mark 4) until the chicken is tender, about 1 hour. Remove the chicken and vegetables on to a serving dish. Discard the bouquet garni. Skim off excess fat from the liquor in the dish. Add the wine. Combine the remaining butter and flour together. Break into small pieces and add to the wine sauce. Stir and warm until it thickens. Cook for 5 minutes. Pour over the chicken. Serve with potatoes and mixed vegetables.

# PORK CHOPS WITH GARLIC SAUCE

METRIC

*4 pork chops*
*50 gm butter*
*1 small onion*
*salt and pepper*

***The sauce***

*50 gm butter*
*25 gm flour*
*1 small onion*
*1 small carrot*
*2 tomatoes*
*2 cloves garlic*
*125 ml beef cube stock*
*½ teaspoon sugar*
*bouquet garni*
*salt and pepper*

IMPERIAL

*4 pork chops*
*2 oz butter*
*1 small onion*
*salt and pepper*

***The sauce***

*2 oz butter*
*1 oz flour*
*1 small onion*
*1 small carrot*
*2 tomatoes*
*2 cloves garlic*
*½ pint beef cube stock*
*½ teaspoon sugar*
*bouquet garni*
*salt and pepper*

**The sauce:** Melt the butter in a saucepan and work in the flour using a wooden spoon. Skin and cut up the onion. Peel and dice the carrot. Immerse the tomatoes in hot water for a few minutes, then skin and cut up. Crush the cloves. Slowly add the stock to the butter/flour roux, stirring to keep the mixture smooth. Add the rest of the ingredients and season. Heat gently until the sauce thickens. Cover and simmer for 1 hour.

**The meat:** While the sauce is cooking, prepare the meat. Melt the butter. Skin and chop up the onion. Fry the pork chops and onions gently for 20 minutes, turning so that the meat cooks evenly. Remove the bouquet garni from the sauce and pour the sauce over the chops.

# LAMB KEBABS

METRIC

*A leg of lamb, 2 - 2½ kilos, boned*

***The sauce***

*3 tablespoons salad oil*

*2 tablespoons vinegar*

*6 sprigs fresh mint*

*2 tablespoons finely chopped onion*

*1 teaspoon salt*

*¼ teaspoon pepper*

*¼ teaspoon paprika*

IMPERIAL

*A leg of lamb, 4 - 5 lb, boned*

***The sauce***

*3 tablespoons salad oil*

*2 tablespoons vinegar*

*6 sprigs fresh mint*

*2 tablespoons finely chopped onion*

*1 teaspoon salt*

*¼ teaspoon pepper*

*¼ teaspoon paprika*

Mix all the ingredients of the sauce together. Remove the fat and gristle from the meat and cut the meat into small, 2.5 cm (1 inch) cubes. Pour the sauce over the meat and place in a refrigerator for 2 - 4 hours. Thread the meat on skewers and grill. Turn frequently and baste with the sauce left from the meat. Pineapple chunks, tomato halves, mushrooms and bacon rolls may be threaded alternately on the skewers with the lamb.

# BEEF KEBABS

METRIC
*1 kg fillet beef*
*100 gm mushroom caps*
*2 medium sized onions*
*fat*
*mustard*

IMPERIAL
*2 lb fillet beef*
*4 oz mushroom caps*
*2 medium sized onions*
*fat*
*mustard*

Cut the beef into 5 cm (2 inch) cubes. Skin and cut the onions into chunks. Place the beef cubes, onions and mushrooms alternately on skewers. Brush with melted fat and mustard to taste. Grill for 4 - 7 minutes.

# LAMB WITH GARLIC AND ROSEMARY

METRIC
*Leg or shoulder of lamb*
*4 cloves garlic*
*4 sprigs rosemary*
*25 gm melted butter*
*1 glass white wine*
*salt and black pepper*

IMPERIAL
*Leg or shoulder of lamb*
*4 cloves garlic*
*4 sprigs rosemary*
*1 oz melted butter*
*1 glass white wine*
*salt and black pepper*

Using a sharp knife, make four incisions in the meat to the bone. Press a clove of garlic and a sprig of rosemary into each cut. Rub the meat with salt and pepper and brush with the butter. Wrap the meat in metal foil and bake in a moderate oven (180°C, 350° F, gas mark 4) allowing 25 minutes per 500 gm (30 minutes per lb). After 50 minutes - 1 hour, remove the foil and continue cooking. 15 minutes before the end of the cooking time pour the wine over the meat. Serve with boiled new potatoes, parsnips and gravy made from the wine liquor from the meat.

# BREAST OF LAMB WITH CELERY STUFFING

METRIC
*1 breast of lamb*
*celery stuffing*
*50 gm butter*
*50 gm breadcrumbs*
*salt and pepper*
***Celery stuffing***
*100 gm breadcrumbs*
*4 stalks celery*
*1 small onion*
*25 gm fat*
*1 teaspoon salt*
*pepper*
*1 teaspoon dried sage*
*1 egg*

IMPERIAL
*1 breast of lamb*
*celery stuffing*
*2 oz butter*
*2 oz breadcrumbs*
*salt and pepper*
***Celery stuffing***
*4 oz breadcrumbs*
*4 stalks celery*
*1 small onion*
*1 oz fat*
*1 teaspoon salt*
*pepper*
*1 teaspoon dried sage*
*1 egg*

Wash and clean the meat, removing as much fat as possible. Make an incision into the meat and fill with celery stuffing. Close with skewers. Coat the lamb with breadcrumbs and season. Melt the fat in the roasting tin. Place the meat in the tin and spoon some fat over it. Bake in a moderate oven (180°C, 350°F, gas mark 4) allowing 25 minutes per 500 gm (30 minutes per lb) until the meat is cooked and tender.
**Celery stuffing:** Clean and dry the celery and cut into small pieces. Skin and chop the onion. Melt the fat in a frying pan and add the celery and onion. Fry gently for a few minutes until the onion softens. Remove from the heat and add the rest of the ingredients. If the mixture is too dry to bind, add a little water.

# IRISH STEW

METRIC

*1 kilo lamb or mutton*
*1½ kilo potatoes*
*1 litre water*
*4 medium sized carrots*
*2 medium sized onions*
*1 small turnip*
*3 tablespoons chopped parsely*
*1 bay leaf*
*salt and pepper*

IMPERIAL

*2½ lb lamb or mutton*
*3 lb potatoes*
*2 pints water*
*4 medium sized carrots*
*2 medium sized onions*
*1 small turnip*
*3 tablespoons chopped parsely*
*1 bay leaf*
*salt and pepper*

Wash the meat and cut into pieces. Remove as much fat as possible. Boil the meat in the water and skim until nearly all the fat is removed from the surface of the liquid. Peel and slice the potatoes, carrots and turnip. Skin and slice the onions. Place a layer of potatoes at the bottom of a large saucepan. Then add a layer of the meat then vegetables and then potatoes. Continue until all the ingredients are used up, seasoning each layer as it is formed. Pour over the liquid in which the meat was boiled and add the bay leaf. Cover with a lid and simmer very gently for 1 ½ - 2 hours. Serve hot.

# BEEF GOULASH

METRIC

*400 gm stewing beef*
*300 gm potatoes*
*1 clove garlic*
*2 onions*
*15 gm fat*
*2 teaspoons paprika*
*1 teaspoon salt*
*pinch pepper*
*2 beef stock cubes*
*500 ml water*
***Dumplings***
*150 gm self raising flour*
*½ level teaspoon salt*
*25 gm butter*
*1 level teaspoon caraway seeds*

IMPERIAL

*1 lb stewing beef*
*12 oz potatoes*
*1 clove garlic*
*2 onions*
*½ oz fat*
*2 teaspoons paprika*
*1 teaspoon salt*
*pinch pepper*
*2 beef stock cubes*
*1 pint water*
***Dumplings***
*6 oz self raising flour*
*½ level teaspoon salt*
*1 oz butter*
*1 level teaspoon caraway seeds*

Cut the meat into cubes and brown in the fat. Crush the garlic, skin and slice the onions. Add the garlic, onions and seasoning to the meat. Dissolve the beef cubes in hot water and pour over the meat. Cover and simmer for 2 ½ hours. Peel and dice the potatoes. Add to the stew. Add more water if necessary and simmer until the potatoes are cooked. Taste for seasoning. Serve hot with caraway dumplings.

**Dumplings:** Sift the flour and salt together. Rub in the butter until the mixture looks like breadcrumbs. Stir in the caraway seeds. Add enough water to make a soft dough and form into 12 small balls. Flour the balls and your hands to prevent the mixture from sticking. Drop the dumplings gently into boiling water and boil for 25 minutes.

# GOULASH EN CASSEROLE

| METRIC | IMPERIAL |
|---|---|
| *1 kilo chuck steak* | *2 lb chuck steak* |
| *2 medium sized onions* | *2 medium sized onions* |
| *75 gm lard* | *3 oz lard* |
| *200 gm can tomato sauce* | *8 oz can tomato sauce* |
| *400 gm tomatoes* | *1 lb tomatoes* |
| *1 tablespoon flour* | *1 tablespoon flour* |
| *1 tablespoon paprika* | *1 tablespoon paprika* |
| *2 bouillon cubes* | *2 bouillon cubes* |
| *1 clove garlic* | *1 clove garlic* |
| *1 bouquet garni* | *1 bouquet garni* |
| *1½ level teaspoons salt* | *1½ level teaspoons salt* |
| *250 ml water* | *½ pint water* |

Cut the meat into small cubes, skin and slice the onions. Fry the meat and onions in the fat until the onions are softened. Work in the flour using a wooden spoon. Dissolve the bouillon cubes in the water and pour over the meat. Crush the clove of garlic. Skin and dice the tomatoes. Add all the ingredients to the meat and turn into a warmed casserole dish. Cover and bake in a moderate oven (180°C, 350°F, gas mark 4) for 1½ hours until the meat is tender. Remove the bouquet garni. Serve with hot macaroni.

# MEAT BALLS

METRIC

*670 gm lean steak*
*25 gm breadcrumbs*
*25 gm Parmesan cheese*
*1 egg*
*½ teaspoon basil*
*3 tablespoons water*
*salt and pepper*
*15 gm fat for frying*
***The sauce***
*1 medium sized onion*
*1 clove garlic*
*two 350 gm tin tomatoes*
*one 125 gm tin concentrated tomato purée*
*2 tablespoons chopped parsley*
*1 teaspoon dried marjoram*
*1 teaspoon salt*

*IMPERIAL*

*1½ lb lean steak*
*1 oz breadcrumbs*
*1 oz Parmesan cheese*
*1 egg*
*½ teaspoon basil*
*3 tablespoons water*
*salt and pepper*
*½ oz fat for frying*
***The sauce***
*1 medium sized onion*
*1 clove garlic*
*two 14 oz tin tomatoes*
*one 5 oz tin concentrated tomato purée*
*2 tablespoons chopped parsley*
*1 teaspoon dried marjoram*
*1 teaspoon salt*

Finely mince the meat, two or three times if necessary. Beat the egg and grate the cheese. Blend the meat, breadcrumbs, eggs, cheese, water and basil together, seasoning with salt and pepper to taste. Shape into balls 2.5 - 4 cm (1-1½ inches) in diameter. Melt the fat in a frying pan and add the meat balls. Cook gently. When brown, pour the sauce over them, cover and simmer for 1½ - 2 hours, stirring occasionally.
**The sauce:** skin and chop the onion. Skin and crush the garlic. Blend all the ingredients of the sauce together.

# SAVORY BROAD BEANS

METRIC
*400 gm broad beans, shelled*
*12 spring onions*
*15 gm butter*
*1 rasher streaky bacon, lightly fried and rinded*
*1 clove garlic*
*1 teaspoon chopped parsley*
*1 teaspoon chopped savory*
*2 tablespoons cream*
*salt and pepper*

IMPERIAL
*1 lb broad beans, shelled*
*12 spring onions*
*½ oz butter*
*1 rasher streaky bacon, lightly fried and rinded*
*1 clove garlic*
*1 teaspoon chopped parsley*
*1 teaspoon chopped savory*
*2 tablespoons cream*
*salt and pepper*

Cook the beans in salted water until tender. Cut the onions into small pieces including some of the green tops and crush the garlic. Melt the butter in a pan and add the onions and garlic. Heat gently until the onions soften. Drain the beans and keep warm. Add 4 tablespoons of the liquor from the beans to the pan. Cut up the bacon and add with the herbs to the pan. Add salt and pepper to taste. Remove the clove of garlic and remove the pan from the heat. Stir in the cream. Warm but do not boil. Add the beans.

*Savory*

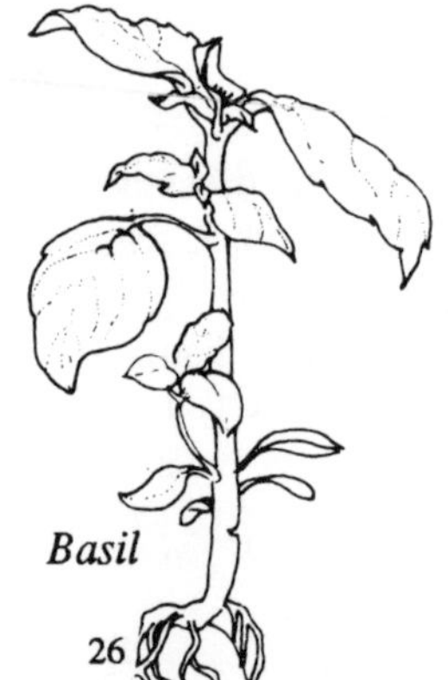

*Basil*

*Thyme*

# HORSERADISH CREAM

METRIC
*2 tablespoons grated horseradish*
*2 teaspoons lemon juice*
*2 teaspoons sugar*
*pinch mustard*
*125 ml cream*

IMPERIAL
*2 tablespoons grated horseradish*
*2 teaspoons lemon juice*
*2 teaspoons sugar*
*pinch mustard*
*¼ pint cream*

Whip the cream until it just ‘trails’. Mix the other ingredients together. Fold into the cream. Serve with beef.

# CHEESE POTATOES

METRIC
*8 large potatoes*
*50 gm butter*
*50 gm Cheddar cheese*
*2 tablespoons chopped chives*
*1 teaspoon salt*
*pinch paprika*

IMPERIAL
*8 large potatoes*
*2 oz butter*
*2 oz Cheddar cheese*
*2 tablespoons chopped chives*
*1 teaspoon salt*
*pinch paprika*

Cook the potatoes in their jackets. Melt the butter and add the cheese, chives and seasonings. Remove the tops of the potatoes and scoop out some of the insides. Mix the potatoes with the cheese mixture and then pile on top of each potato. Serve alone or with cooked ham.

# OMELETTE AUX FINES HERBES

METRIC
*2 eggs*
*15 gm butter*
*½ teaspoon each chopped parsley and chives*
*pinch tarragon and chervil*
*2 tablespoons water*
*salt and pepper*

IMPERIAL
*2 eggs*
*½ oz butter*
*½ teaspoon each chopped parsley and chives*
*pinch tarragon and chervil*
*2 tablespoons water*
*salt and pepper*

Beat the eggs lightly. Add the water, herbs and seasoning. Mix well. Melt the butter in a small frying pan. Pour the egg mixture into the pan, tilting the pan to let the mixture spread. Gently stir the mixture drawing in the sides of the omelette. As soon as the egg is set, stop stirring and leave over a medium heat until the underside is brown. Using a palette knife, flick one third of the omelette to the centre and then the other third to the centre. Turn out on to a warm plate.

*Tarragon*

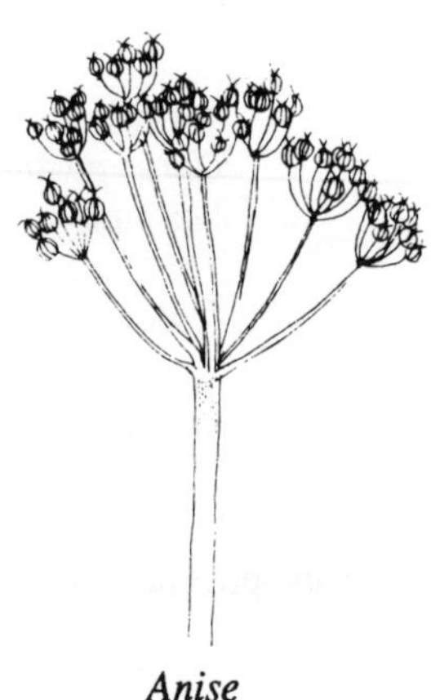

*Anise*

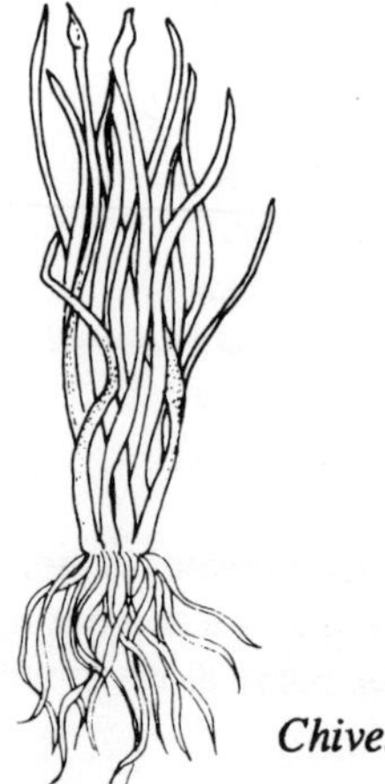

*Chives*

# MARRROW SOUFFLÉ

METRIC
*400 gm marrow*
***The sauce***
*50 gm butter*
*25 gm flour*
*250 ml milk*
*3 eggs*
*100 gm cheese*
*2 teaspoons summer savory*
*salt and pepper*

IMPERIAL
*1 lb marrow*
***The sauce***
*2 oz butter*
*1 oz flour*
*½ pint milk*
*3 eggs*
*4 oz cheese*
*2 teaspoons summer savory*
*salt and pepper*

Peel the marrow, slice and remove seeds. Cook in boiling, salted water until tender but still firm. Drain and cut into chunks. Melt the butter and work in the flour using a wooden spoon. Stir in the milk. Season with salt and pepper. Pour half the sauce over the marrow and add the savory to the marrow mixture. Pour into a greased 17 cm (7 inch) soufflé dish. Separate the eggs and grate the cheese. Add the egg yolks and cheese to the remaining white sauce. Beat the egg whites lightly and fold into the cheese sauce. Spoon on top of the marrow. Bake at the top of a fairly hot oven (190°C, 375°F, gas mark 5) for 30 minutes, until risen and golden brown.

# TOMATO RING

METRIC

*400 gm tomatoes*
*2 small onions*
*1 small clove garlic*
*1 tablespoon unflavoured gelatine*
*1 teaspoon sugar*
*2 peppercorns*
*1 bay leaf*
*1 tablespoon tarragon vinegar*
*3 tablespoons lemon juice*
*½ teaspoon salt*

IMPERIAL

*1 lb tomatoes*
*2 small onions*
*1 small clove garlic*
*1 tablespoon unflavoured gelatine*
*1 teaspoon sugar*
*2 peppercorns*
*1 bay leaf*
*1 tablespoon tarragon vinegar*
*3 tablespoons lemon juice*
*½ teaspoon salt*

Soften the gelatine in cold water for 5 minutes. Immerse the tomatoes in hot water. Remove skins and quarter. Cover with water. Skin and dice the onions. Skin and crush the garlic clove. Tie the bay leaf and peppercorns in a piece of muslin. Cook the tomatoes with the onions, garlic, herbs and salt until the onions have softened. Place the gelatine in a 500 ml (1 pint) measure. Remove the muslin bag and pour the hot tomato mixture on to the gelatine. Add the vinegar and lemon juice. Make up to 500 ml (1 pint) if necessary with water. When beginning to set, pour into a ring mould. When firm, turn out on to a bed of watercress or lettuce. Serve with cold chicken or poached salmon.

# TOMATO SALAD

METRIC
*4 tomatoes*
*oil and vinegar dressing*
*2 teaspoons freshly chopped basil or chives*
***The dressing***
*1 tablespoon vinegar*
*3 tablespoons olive oil*
*½ teaspoon salt*
*¼ teaspoon black pepper*

IMPERIAL
*4 tomatoes*
*oil and vinegar dressing*
*2 teaspoons freshly chopped basil or chives*
***The dressing***
*1 tablespoon vinegar*
*3 tablespoons olive oil*
*½ teaspoon salt*
*¼ teaspoon black pepper*

Immerse the tomatoes in hot water for a few minutes. Skin and slice. Place in oil and vinegar dressing and leave to stand for 30 minutes. Remove the tomato slices. Serve in individual dishes sprinkled with basil or chives.
**The dressing:** Mix all the ingredients together and shake or mix thoroughly.

# COS LETTUCE SALAD

METRIC
*1 lettuce*
*1 teaspoon each chopped tarragon, chervil and chives*
*French dressing*

IMPERIAL
*1 lettuce*
*1 teaspoon each chopped tarragon, chervil and chives*
*French dressing*

Wash and dry the lettuce. Cut the leaves and place a layer of lettuce leaves in a bowl. Sprinkle herbs and dressing over the lettuce. Cover with a further layer of lettuce. Season. Repeat until all the lettuce is used up.

# FRENCH DRESSING

METRIC
*125 ml vegetable oil*
*3 tablespoons malt vinegar*
*1 teaspoon sugar*
*¼ teaspoon dry mustard*
*pinch ground pepper*
*¼ teaspoon paprika*
*½ teaspoon salt*

IMPERIAL
*¼ pint vegetable oil*
*3 tablespoons malt vinegar*
*1 teaspoon sugar*
*¼ teaspoon dry mustard*
*pinch ground pepper*
*¼ teaspoon paprika*
*½ teaspoon salt*

Place all the ingredients in a bowl and mix thoroughly using a fork or electric beater. Store in a refrigerator.

# COTTAGE CHEESE FRENCH DRESSING

METRIC
*Ingredients as for French Dressing*
*75 gm cottage cheese*

IMPERIAL
*Ingredients as for French Dressing*
*3 oz cottage cheese*

Add the cheese to the French dressing, and mix in.

# CUCUMBER FRENCH DESSING

METRIC
*Ingredients as for French dressing*
*100 gm grated cucumber (well drained)*

IMPERIAL
*Ingredients as for French dressing*
*4 oz grated cucumber (well drained)*

Add the cucumber to the French dressing and mix in.

# SALAD DRESSING

METRIC
*25 gm flour*
*37 gm castor sugar*
*25 gm butter*
*1 teaspoon salt*
*¾ teaspoon dry mustard*
*¼ teaspoon powdered rosemary*
*¼ teaspoon powdered savory*
*pinch powdered thyme*
*2 eggs, lightly beaten*
*150 ml milk*
*2 tablespoons lemon juice or vinegar*
*3 tablespoons single cream (optional)*

IMPERIAL
*1 oz flour*
*1½ oz castor sugar*
*1 oz butter*
*1 teaspoon salt*
*¾ teaspoon dry mustard*
*¼ teaspoon powdered rosemary*
*¼ teaspoon powdered savory*
*pinch powdered thyme*
*2 eggs, lightly beaten*
*¼ pint milk*
*2 tablespoons lemon juice or vinegar*
*3 tablespoons single cream (optional)*

Sift the dry ingredients together in the top of a double boiler. Add the eggs and milk slowly, mixing well. Stir in the lemon juice or vinegar. Cook over boiling water, stirring constantly until the mixture thickens. Add the butter and stir until blended. Strain, cool and then chill. Add the cream. Cover and store in a cool place.

# LOW CALORIE SALAD DRESSING

METRIC

*250 ml tomato juice*
*2½ tablespoons vegetable oil*
*1 tablespoon Worcestershire sauce*
*2 tablespoons vinegar*
*1 small onion*
*2 tablespoons chopped parsley*
*¼ teaspoon salt*
*¼ teaspoon black pepper*

IMPERIAL

*½ pint tomato juice*
*2 ½ tablespoons vegetable oil*
*1 tablespoon Worcestershire sauce*
*2 tablespoons vinegar*
*1 small onion*
*2 tablespoons chopped parsley*
*¼ teaspoon salt*
*¼ teaspoon black pepper*

Combine all the ingredients. Cool thoroughly. Shake well before serving.

# BOUQUET GARNI

METRIC

*1 bay leaf*
*1 sprig parsley*
*1 sprig thyme*
*2 or 3 peppercorns (optional)*

IMPERIAL

*1 bay leaf*
*1 sprig parsley*
*1 sprig thyme*
*2 or 3 peppercorns (optional)*

The bunches of herbs and spices are tied up in a small muslin bag and removed after cooking. Used in a wide range of dishes and the herbs used may be varied.

# CINNAMON APPLE CRUMBLE

METRIC
*400 gm cooking apples*
*75 gm castor sugar*
*50 gm digestive biscuits*
*25 gm demerara sugar*
*1 tablespoon water*
*1 teaspoon cinnamon*

IMPERIAL
*1 lb cooking apples*
*3 oz castor sugar*
*2 oz digestive biscuits*
*1 oz demerara sugar*
*1 tablespoon water*
*1 teaspoon cinnamon*

Peel, core and slice the apples. Place in a saucepan with the castor sugar and cinnamon. Bring to the boil and simmer until soft. Beat well and leave to cool. Turn into a pie dish. Crush the digestive biscuits and mix with the demerara sugar. Place on top of the apple mixture.

*Rosemary*

*Coriander*

*Sage*

# MINCEMEAT

METRIC

*400 gm shredded suet*
*400 gm peeled, cored, finely chopped cooking apples*
*400 gm currants*
*400 gm stoned raisins*
*200 gm sultanas*
*400 gm demerara sugar*
*300 gm mixed peel*
*2 lemons*
*½ teaspoon each ground nutmeg, ground mace, ground cinnamon, allspice*
*6 tablespoons brandy or whisky or rum*

IMPERIAL

*1 lb shredded suet*
*1 lb peeled, cored, finely chopped cooking apples*
*1 lb currants*
*1 lb stoned raisins*
*8 oz sultanas*
*1 lb demerara sugar*
*12 oz mixed peel*
*2 lemons*
*½ teaspoon each ground nutmeg, ground mace, ground cinnamon, allspice*
*6 tablespoons brandy or whisky or rum*

If necessary wash the fruit but the fruit must be thoroughly dry. Grate the rind from the lemons and squeeze out the lemon juice from the fruit. Mix all the ingredients together. Stir thoroughly. Pot in sterilised jars, fill each to the top and seal with waxed paper. Be sure that no air is trapped under the paper. Close the jars with airtight covers and store in a cool place. If any bubbles are formed at the top of the jars during storage, then the mincemeat is starting to ferment. Remove from the jars into a large pan. Stirring carefully, bring the mixture to the boil for 1 minute and then repot in fresh, sterilized jars.

# DARK FRUIT CAKE

METRIC

*175 gm flour*
*75 gm butter*
*100 gm brown sugar*
*4 eggs*
*4 tablespoons black treacle*
*6 tablespoons apple juice, or rum or brandy or sherry*
*400 gm stoned raisins*
*200 gm crystallised cherries*
*200 gm citron thinly sliced*
*200 gm figs or dates*
*75 gm candied orange peel*
*75 gm candied lemon peel*
*¼ teaspoon bicarbonate of soda*
*½ teaspoon each mixed spice, cinnamon, nutmeg, salt*

IMPERIAL

*7 oz flour*
*3 oz butter*
*4 oz brown sugar*
*4 eggs*
*4 tablespoons black treacle*
*6 tablespoons apple juice, or rum or brandy or sherry*
*1 lb stoned raisins*
*8 oz crystallised cherries*
*8 oz citron thinly sliced*
*8 oz figs or dates*
*3 oz candied orange peel*
*3 oz candied lemon peel*
*¼ teaspoon bicarbonate of soda*
*½ teaspoon each mixed spice, cinnamon, nutmeg, salt*

Dredge the fruit in a little of the flour. Sift together the rest of the flour, bicarbonate of soda, spices and salt. Cream the butter and sugar. Separate the eggs and beat the egg yolks. Add the flour mixture and fruit juice or liquor alternately, mixing well. Beat egg whites until stiff and fold into the batter. Add the dredged fruits and mix evenly. Line 1 large or 2 medium-sized loaf tins with three thicknesses of greaseproof paper. Fill the tin or tins three-quarters full. Cover with three thicknesses of greaseproof paper. Steam for 3 hours. Remove the top paper covering and bake in a very slow oven (130°C, 250°F, gas mark ½) for 2 hours. Turn out on to a wire tray to cool. Store in aluminium foil in an airtight container in a cool place.

# SEED CAKE

METRIC

*200 gm self raising flour*
*100 gm butter*
*100 gm castor sugar*
*25 gm caraway seeds*
*pinch salt*
*2 eggs*
*milk to mix*

IMPERIAL

*8 oz self raising flour*
*4 oz butter*
*4 oz castor sugar*
*1 oz caraway seeds*
*pinch salt*
*2 eggs*
*milk to mix*

Sieve the flour and salt together. Rub in the butter until the mixture looks like breadcrumbs. Stir in the sugar and caraway seeds. Beat the eggs and a little milk. Work into the flour mixture, adding enough milk to give a soft, dropping consistency. Line a greased 17.5 cm (7 inch) tin with greased greaseproof paper. Bake in a moderate oven (180°C, 350°F, gas mark 4) for 1 - 1¼ hours until firm to the touch and cooked through.

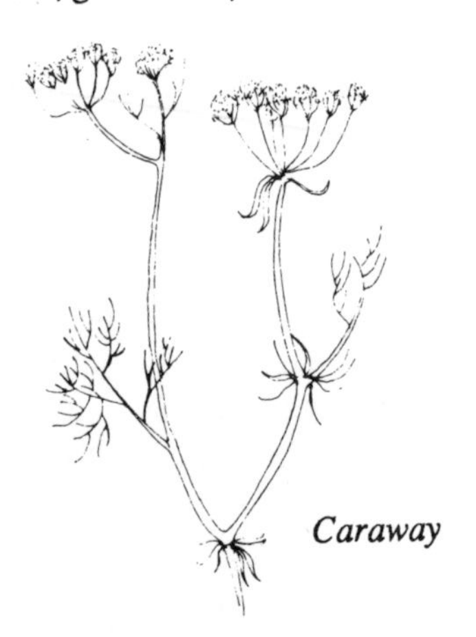

*Caraway*

*Dill*

*Mint*

# CARAWAY SCONES

METRIC
*200 gm self-raising flour*
*50 gm butter*
*25 gm castor sugar*
*pinch salt*
*2 level teaspoons caraway seeds*
*1 large egg - beaten*
*1 or 2 tablespoons milk*

IMPERIAL
*8 oz self-raising flour*
*2 oz butter*
*1 oz castor sugar*
*pinch salt*
*2 level teaspoons caraway seeds*
*1 large egg - beaten*
*1 or 2 tablespoons milk*

Sift the flour and salt together. Rub in the butter until the mixture resembles breadcrumbs. Stir in the sugar and caraway seeds. Add the egg and enough milk to form a soft light dough. Roll out to a thickness of 1 cm ( ½ inch) on a floured board. Cut into rounds and bake in a greased baking sheet in the centre of a hot oven (230°C, 450°F, gas mark 8) for 10 - 15 minutes.

# CINNAMON SCONES

Replace caraway seeds in the above recipe by ½ teaspoon of cinnamon. Sift the cinnamon with the flour and salt.

# CARAWAY SEED BISCUITS

METRIC
*300 gm flour*
*100 gm butter*
*100 gm caster sugar*
*2 teaspoons baking powder*
*1 egg, well beaten*
*2 tablespoons milk*
*1 teaspoon vanilla or*
*½ teaspoon cinnamon*
*2 teaspoons caraway seeds*

IMPERIAL
*12 oz flour*
*4 oz butter*
*4 oz caster sugar*
*2 teaspoons baking powder*
*1 egg, well beaten*
*2 tablespoons milk*
*1 teaspoon vanilla or*
*½ teaspoon cinnamon*
*2 teaspoons caraway seeds*

Cream the butter and sugar. Add the beaten egg, vanilla or cinnamon and milk. Sift 250 gm (10 oz) of the flour and the other dry ingredients together. Stir into the butter mixture. Then add enough of the remaining flour to make the dough firm enough to handle. Roll out on a floured board to a thickness of 0.5 cm ( ¼ inch). Cut into shapes and place on an ungreased baking sheet, brush with beaten egg and a little sugar. Cook in a moderate oven (190°C, 375°F, gas mark 5) for 10 - 15 minutes.

# CINNAMON BISCUITS

METRIC
*100 gm plain flour*
*½ teaspoon cinnamon*
*½ teaspoon baking powder*
*100 gm butter*

IMPERIAL
*4 oz plain flour*
*½ teaspoon cinnamon*
*½ teaspoon baking powder*
*4 oz butter*

| METRIC | IMPERIAL |
| --- | --- |
| *75 gm caster sugar* | *3 oz caster sugar* |
| *75 gm desiccated coconut* | *3 oz desiccated coconut* |
| *1 egg* | *1 egg* |

Sift the flour, cinnamon and baking powder together. Rub in the butter until the mixture looks like breadcrumbs. Stir in the caster sugar and coconut. Lightly beat the egg and use to bind the mixture to make a firm dough. Roll out to a thickness of 5 mm (¼) inch. Cut into rounds and place on a greased baking sheet. Bake in a moderate oven (180°C, 350°F, gas mark 4) for 15 minutes.

# GINGER BISCUITS

| METRIC | IMPERIAL |
| --- | --- |
| *500 gm flour* | *20 oz flour* |
| *200 gm butter* | *8 oz butter* |
| *300 gm brown sugar* | *12 oz brown sugar* |
| *2 eggs* | *2 eggs* |
| *6 tablespoons dark treacle* | *6 tablespoons dark treacle* |
| *3 teaspoons bicarbonate of soda* | *3 teaspoons bicarbonate of soda* |
| *3 teaspoons ground ginger* | *3 teaspoons ground ginger* |
| *½ teaspoon salt* | *½ teaspoon salt* |
| *1 teaspoon vinegar* | *1 teaspoon vinegar* |

Sift the flour, bicarbonate of soda, salt and ginger together. Cream the fat and sugar. Beat the eggs lightly and add to the creamed mixture. Add the vinegar and syrup. Mix in the flour mixture. Form into small balls using about 1 tablespoonful of the dough for each. Flatten with the palm of the hand. Cook on a baking sheet in a fairly hot oven (200°C, 400°F, gas mark 6) for 12 to 15 minutes. The biscuits are soft when just cooked but harden on cooling.

# HERB FRENCH OR ITALIAN BREAD

METRIC
*50 gm butter*
*50 gm chopped parsley*
*25 gm finely chopped spring onions*
*2 finely chopped garlic cloves*
*1 long loaf*

IMPERIAL
*2 oz butter*
*2 oz chopped parsley*
*1 oz finely chopped spring onions*
*2 finely chopped garlic cloves*
*1 long loaf*

Soften the butter and mix in the parsley, onions and garlic. Cut the loaf in half lengthwise and spread each half with butter. Sandwich together and wrap in foil. Heat in a warm oven.

# GARLIC BREAD STICKS

METRIC
*100 gm butter*
*2 cloves garlic*
*12 Italian bread sticks or sticks cut from a stale loaf*

IMPERIAL
*4 oz butter*
*2 cloves garlic*
*12 Italian bread sticks or sticks cut from a stale loaf*

Melt the butter and add the cloves of garlic. Leave to stand for 15 minutes and then remove the garlic. Spread on the bread.

# GARLIC BUTTER

METRIC
*100 gm butter*
*1 or 2 cloves*

IMPERIAL
*4 oz butter*
*1 or 2 cloves*

Mash the garlic and cream with the butter.

# ONION BUTTER

METRIC
*100 gm butter*
*1 small bunch spring onions*

IMPERIAL
*4 oz butter*
*1 small bunch spring onions*

Chop the onions finely, including some of the tops and mix with the creamed butter.

# HERB BUTTER

METRIC
*100 gm butter*
*2 tablespoons rosemary, tarragon or basil*
*slice of onion*

IMPERIAL
*4 oz butter*
*2 tablespoons rosemary, tarragon or basil*
*slice of onion*

Cut the onion up finely. Cream all the ingredients together.

# CHEESE - PARSLEY BUTTER

METRIC
*100 gm butter*
*25 gm grated Cheddar, Gruyère*
*or Emmethal cheese*
*1 tablespoon parsley*

IMPERIAL
*4 oz butter*
*1 oz grated Cheddar, Gruyère*
*or Emmethal cheese*
*1 tablespoon parsley*

Cream all the ingredients together.

# MINT TEA

For 1 glass

| METRIC | IMPERIAL |
|---|---|
| *3 teaspoons freshly-chopped* | *3 teaspoons freshly-chopped* |
| *common or pineapple mint or* | *common or pineapple mint or* |
| *1 teaspoon dried mint* | *1 teaspoon dried mint* |
| *250 ml boiling water* | *½ pint boiling water* |
| *sugar* | *sugar* |

Pour the boiling water over the mint. Leave to stand for 5 minutes. Strain. Add sugar to taste. Serve hot or iced garnished with lemon slices.

Anise, borage, lemon balm, sweet marjoram, rosemary and sage teas may be made in the same way. Serve hot or iced, sweetened with honey or sugar or with slices of lemon.

# MINT COOLER

| METRIC | IMPERIAL |
|---|---|
| *3 parts gin* | *3 parts gin* |
| *1 part green crème de menthe* | *1 part green crème de menthe* |
| *soda water* | *soda water* |
| *slice of orange* | *slice of orange* |
| *1 sprig mint* | *1 sprig mint* |

Fill a tall glass with ice cubes. Add the gin and crème de menthe. Fill with soda water. Decorate with a slice of orange, a cherry and a sprig of mint.

# FRUIT PUNCH

METRIC

*500 ml unsweetened pineapple juice*
*500 ml orange juice*
*500 ml liquid apple*
*500 ml lemonade*
*a selection of fresh fruits such as apples, oranges, grapes, cherries, strawberries and raspberries*
*borage for decoration*

IMPERIAL

*1 pint unsweetened pineapple juice*
*1 pint orange juice*
*1 pint liquid apple*
*1 pint lemonade*
*a selection of fresh fruits such as apples, oranges, grapes, cherries, strawberries and raspberries*
*borage for decoration*

Mix all the liquids in a large bowl and float the fruit, sliced if necessary, on top. Decorate with borage. Serve with ice.

# EGG NOG

METRIC

*1 white of egg*
*1 tablespoon brandy or sherry*
*1 tablespoon cream*
*sugar*
*nutmeg*

IMPERIAL

*1 white of egg*
*1 tablespoon brandy or sherry*
*1 tablespoon cream*
*sugar*
*nutmeg*

Whisk the egg white until stiff. Pour the brandy or sherry into a long glass and add the cream and sugar to taste. Mix well. Stir the egg white into the brandy (or sherry) mixture. Dust with a little ground nutmeg and serve.

# AMERICAN MEASURES

American measures are given by volume and weight using standard cups and spoons.

**US Standard Measuring Spoons and Cups**

1 tablespoon = 3 teaspoons = ½ fluid ounce = 14.2 ml
2 tablespoons = 1 fluid ounce = 28 ml
4 tablespoons = ¼ cup
5 tablespoons = ⅓ cup
8 tablespoons = ½ cup
10 tablespoons = ⅝ cup (i.e. ⅔ approx.)
12 tablespoons = ¾ cup
16 tablespoons = 2 cups = 8 fluid ounces = ½ US pint
32 tablespoons = 2 cups = 16 fluid ounces = 1 US pint.

| Metric (Imperial) | American |
| --- | --- |
| 1 teaspoon | 1 teaspoon |
| 1 tablespoon | 1 tablespoon |
| 1½ teaspoons | 2 tablespoons |
| 2 tablespoons | 3 tablespoons |
| 3 tablespoons | ¼ (scant) cup |
| 4 tablespoons | 5 tablespoons |
| 5 tablespoons | 6 tablespoons |
| 5½ tablespoons | 7 tablespoons |
| 6 tablespoons (scant ¼ pint) | ½ cup |
| ¼ pint | ⅔ cup |
| scant ½ pint | 1 cup |
| ½ pint (10 fl oz) | 1¼ cups |
| ¾ pint (15 fl oz) | scant 2 cups |
| ¾ pint (16 fl oz) | 2 cups (1 pint) |
| 1 pint (20 fl oz) | 2½ cups |

| Metric (Imperial) | American |
| --- | --- |
| ***flour, plain or self-raising*** | |
| 15 gm (½ oz) | 2 tablespoons |
| 25 gm (1 oz) | 1¼ cup |
| 100/125 gm (4 oz) | 1 cup |
| ***sugar, castor or granulated, brown (firmly packed)*** | |
| 15 gm (1 oz) | 2 tablespoons |
| 100/125 gm (4 oz) | ½ cup |
| 200/225 gm (8 oz) | 1 cup |
| ***butter, margarine, fat*** | |
| 1 oz | 2 tablespoons |
| 225 gm (8 oz) | 1 cup |
| 150 gm (5 oz) shredded suet | 1 cup |

***1 cup (American) contains approximately***

100/125 gm (4 oz) grated cheese, 50 gm (2 oz) fresh breadcrumbs, 100 gm (4 oz) dried breadcrumbs,
100/125 gm (4 oz) pickled beetroot, button mushrooms, shelled peas, red/blackcurrants, 5 oz strawberries,
175 gm (6 oz) raisins, currants, sultans, chopped candied peel, stoned dates,
225 gm (8 oz) glacé cherries, 150 gm (5 oz) shelled whole walnuts, 100 gm (4 oz) chopped nuts,
75 gm (3 oz) dessicated coconut,
225 gm (8 oz) cottage cheese,
100/125 gm (4 oz) curry powder,
225 gm (8 oz) minced raw meat,
⅜ pint (7½ fl oz) cream.

# INDEX